WHAT LOVE IS

What Love Is

*Reflections on the True Meaning
& Authentic Practice of Love*

Thom Rutledge

AUTHOR OF THE *GREATER POSSIBILITES*

Cover Photo by Mark Smith

*When it is time to say good bye, if there is just
one photo at my wake, may it be this one. -Thom*

Thom Rutledge
331 22nd Ave North, Suite One
Nashville, TN 37203

thomrutledgeauthor@gmail.com
www.thomrutledge.com

ISBN 978-1542697347

Dedications

For Karen with my sincere apology for blowing up the lab.

For Lisette & Wynn and for Zoe & Brad, as you begin.

For Lorene, Jason & Luekelina because love is strength.

And especially for Dede: To me, you are what love is.

The highest function of love is that it makes the loved one a
unique and irreplaceable being.

— Tom Robbins

Immature love says, "I love you because I need you."
Mature love says, "I need you because I love you."

— Erich Fromm

One cannot be strong without love.

— Paul Tillich

CONTENTS

INTRODUCTION

We teach best what we most need to learn. — Richard Bach

As I write this, I have been on this planet almost 64 years, enough time to have learned a thing or two, maybe even to have accumulated some wisdom. Or, as my therapist often said at the end of our sessions, "Or not."

Somewhere along the way, I became aware that to love someone well takes work. Unfortunately, I had not learned that before my first marriage. As a result, I came up way short, to say the least, for my wife and her two wonderful daughters. I love my life now, the life my current wife and I have created together over these past 30 years, so I have no desire to travel back to change what went before. But I remain very sorry for hurting the three of them.

I did not do so well with my parents, brothers and sister either. I believe I did the best I could at any given time through the years but with the perspective these additional years have given me, I have discovered some regrets. I remind myself that I can have regret without shame – and that helps. And it is important for all of us to be careful to not judge our past selves with our current selves as the standard of measure.

No doubt, my wife, Dede, has been my greatest teacher of what love is. And she and I have certainly been students together, our relationship being the teacher. I will leave it to her to write her own book and tell you about her perspective. I will tell you that, for me, the past 30 years have been exciting, fun, terrifying, enlightening, worrisome, hilarious, entertaining, painful, confusing, more fun, interesting, scary, surprising, fulfilling and I could fill at least a couple more pages with this description. Not sure who I would be, but I would not be this particular version of Thom if Dede and I had not become lab partners through this strange experiment called life. Whether our coming together was a happy accident or our relationship was planned from the beginning, I am filled with gratitude for what we have. And Dede is too. She told me so – just yesterday, in fact.

My work as a psychotherapist has also been a primary source of my learning about love. That could most certainly fill another book (that I probably should write) but for now, I will paraphrase the words of the innovative physician/healer, Patch Adams: everybody is a teacher and everybody is a student. Doing my best

to figure out how to help other people with love –
difficulties in relationships and terrible difficulties
with loving themselves – has afforded me the
opportunity to actually work on learning about
love for a living. Not a bad job if you can get it.

I did not realize it at the beginning of this project
but *What Love is* is the second book in a series that
is taking shape as I write. The first, The Greater
Possibilities, was released last year. And my plan is
to have the third in the series ready to roll out next
year.

So, for now we land on this book. Simple and
straightforward. I hope you will find it thought-
provoking, instructive, challenging, reassuring and
entertaining. I have written this as a gift book and
hope that you will like it enough to want to share
it. Gift book or not, I have not written some
namby-pamby book of cliché aphorisms and
happy affirmations. I have written this book to
genuinely share some of what I have learned about
love.

This is no comprehensive treatise on the nature of
– or the practice of – love. These are my thoughts,
my reflections; these are lessons I have learned
along the way. One of the many slogans from
Alcoholics Anonymous applies here: Take what is

helpful and leave what is not. I do hope you will find something useful here. Thank you for reading. Let me know what you think.

–Thom Rutledge / October 2017

The Most Important Thing

Discovery is meaningless without action. — TR

I can take guitar lessons from Eric Clapton but if I don't practice between lessons, I will not play the guitar. I can show up faithfully for my lessons, I can pay close attention and I will be able to genuinely claim that I know a lot about playing the guitar. But without practice, what I know will not change the fact that I cannot play.

You can understand everything there is to understand in this little book and it will not make the slightest difference in how you love.

Please read what follows with the intention of creating a daily practice of what you discover to be useful here. Practice is the only way to change. And commitment to perpetual practice is the only way to mastery.

Practice makes...practice.

Words

The only thing that lives forever is love.
- Elisabeth Kübler-Ross

The Language of Love

I love you. I love you so much. I love you so very much. You mean everything to me. I would cut off my right arm for you. You are the sun and the moon and the stars. And on and on. Such is the language of love, the magnificent language of romance.

Delivering

It is a beautiful language, no doubt. And it is a beneficial language – or is it? Well, that depends on who is speaking the language of love. Specifically, it depends on whether or not the person doing the talking will stand behind his or her words. It's one thing to promise your right arm and quite another to actually deliver.

Love is a deeply felt emotion.
Love is a powerful motivator.
Love must be demonstrated.

Universally Misunderstood

There is no more universal idea than that of love. It is one thing we can all understand and yet it is probably the most commonly misunderstood concept of all time.

Questions

We ask ourselves about love: Do I love her? Do I love him? Does he love me? Does she love me? And we ask each other about love: Do you love me?

There are some questions we can spend a lifetime answering.

The Question

These are all perfectly good questions, but to ensure that the answers to these questions are not "just words," romantic or not, we will all do well to ask one more very important question:

What is love?

Action

*What you do speaks so loudly that I
cannot hear what you say.*

-Ralph Waldo Emerson

Best Place

First, love is more about action than about feeling. It is more about what we do than what we say. This is not an indictment of the language of love, for these expressions are beautiful and make the world a better place to be.

What makes the world the *best* place to be are the acts of love.

Acts of Love

The acts of love are as varied as we are as individuals. What says, "I love you" to one person may mean little or nothing to another. It is important not to assume that what feels loving to you is what will feel loving to your partner. Maybe it will; maybe it won't.

Ask

There is an amazing magical technique that will reveal to you the best ways to express love to your partner. It is frequently overlooked and commonly thought to be "unromantic." Nothing could be farther from the truth.

Here is the amazing magical technique: ASK QUESTIONS. Whatever you do, don't keep this one a secret. Let's tell the world!

Listen

So we ask, "What are the actions – what are my actions – that will let you know that I love you?"

And then we invoke another powerful technique. A technique that is, for far too many people, long forgotten, a practice that is as powerful as any on this earth but one that is overlooked and neglected countless times every day.

It is the practice of listening.

Ask, Listen, Repeat

We ask the question: "What can I do to let you know how much I love you?"

And we listen to the answer. No, we listen for the answers (plural). This is not a question with one or two answers. This is a question that we can spend a lifetime asking each other - and answering.

Asking and listening. Asking and listening. Asking and listening. Asking and...

A daily practice of asking and listening – that's what love is.

Simple Is Not Easy

Do not make the mistake of thinking that just because this is simple, it is an easy thing to do.

Simple does not mean easy.

Sometimes we walk right past simple because we are convinced that anything valuable must be complex.

Maybe, Maybe Not

Maybe your partner loves to be surprised with a bouquet of flowers. But maybe not.

Maybe your partner would much rather you take the time for a walk.

Maybe remembering to vacuum the living room is what love is.

Speak

Do not forget that speaking is an action.

Do not forget to speak your love out loud. "In my family, we didn't talk like that," someone might say. Well... this is an excellent time to begin.

Recognizing that you are not comfortable doing something is a place to begin, not an excuse to stop.

Congruence

Expressing love aloud must always be congruent with your behavior. Empty words are not just useless, they can be very harmful.

Congruence is essential in a healthy loving relationship and we are each responsible for our own congruence. Loving words with loving deeds, that's what love is.

Amends

When you fall short, when you forget to act with love, apology is good. But amends are much better. The word amend means "to change" – much more than apology.

Apology with amends is congruence.

Saying what you mean and meaning what you say – that's what love is.
Love is truthful.

So…

Act with love.

Don't assume, ask questions.

When you ask, listen and put what you
learn into action.

Speak your love out loud and of course,
back that up with action.

When you are wrong, apologize and then
change.

All simple, seldom easy.

Willingness

"But I thought you loved me for who I am"
"I do. But I still need you to be willing to change."

When we refuse to change, we refuse to grow. When we refuse to grow, love suffocates. Willingness to grow, understanding that willingness to change is strength, not weakness - that's what love is.

Imperfections

The art of love is largely the art of persistence.

-Albert Ellis

Curiosity

Being curious is a powerful way to express respect. It is very easy to forget to be curious about our partners when we have been together for some time. Remind yourself to be curious. Don't listen to the voice in your head that says you can know a person better than they can know themselves. That is ridiculous.

Double Check

Even if you are sure that you know what your partner is thinking or feeling, show respect by double checking. "I think that you are upset about what I said yesterday. Are you?"

Be curious. Demonstrate respect with curiosity. That's what love is.

Sometimes when we are absolutely certain about something, we are wrong.

Reliability

Love is not perfect. At least love between human beings is not perfect because we are so radically imperfect ourselves. Do not try to be perfect. Do not try to love perfectly. Instead, be consistent and reliable and flexible.

Being consistent and reliable is a wonderful expression of love. It is a way to let someone know that they matter, that they are important to you.

Show Up

Put your work down and show up for that special occasion. Even better, put your work down and show up for dinner -- just because it is Wednesday.

One of the most loving things anyone can say is, "I am right here."

Pay Attention

Take your blinders off and look around at your world. See your partner there. Pay attention to what they might need from you or what they might want. Do not neglect yourself but neither neglect your partner.

Motivation, Not Excuse

Understanding that no one is perfect should never be used as an excuse when you fall short. Knowing that we are imperfect needs to become a part of our motivation to do our best and to honestly acknowledge when we blow it.

Admitting when we are wrong and not making excuses, that's what love is.

Helpful Fear & Guilt

Normal, healthy emotions will help us to correct course. Fear of hurting someone can improve our judgment. Guilt for hurting someone can inform our amends.

Healthy fear and guilt will guide us
to do better, to be better.
We need to listen.

All Three

There must be room enough for both of you in your relationship. If that is not so, make it so.

This is not about, "Are we going to live your life or my life?" And it is not all just our life. It is all three.

In a healthy relationship, there are three lives: your life, my life & our life.

Respecting each other's individuality and caring for your relationship together, that's what love is.

So...

Be present, show up.
Be consistent. Be reliable.
Acknowledge imperfection.

Remain open, curious and willing to change and to grow - even when running and hiding seems like a good idea, that's what love is. Not running away, that's what love is.

Learning

Love is about learning. Learning about your partner. Learning about yourself. Learning to create a place – physically and emotionally – that is big enough for both of you.

The Work

*The single biggest problem in communication is the illusion
that it has taken place.*
-George Bernard Shaw

Room for Two

Love should support both people's dreams. There will be plenty of opportunities for compromise but compromise should never be about giving up something that is essential for you.

It is delusional to think that everything in your relationship will be 50/50. Of course not.

Being sure there is plenty of room for both of you – that will keep you busy.

Stretch

Love involves flexibility too. It is so easy to become set in our ways - of behaving and of thinking. Sometimes we even become control freaks, not because we want to but because we are just not paying enough attention to prevent rigidity from setting in.

Our personalities are like muscles: they need to be stretched; they need exercise. There is no better exercise for a personality than a relationship.

Endless Opportunity

Get into a relationship and the opportunities for growth are endless. In fact, sometimes being in a relationship is quite exhausting.

Okay, it may be more than sometimes.

Whenever you feel stuck, it is time to look for opportunities to step outside your comfort zone.

Better and Worse

When you are exhausted, be careful to not mistake your fatigue for a loss of love. Maybe the vows should be, "For better and for worse and for all things in between."

Relationships are much harder work than what Hollywood has taught us. Catch your breath, remember that you and your partner are on the same side. You both want the same thing.

You will know you are outside your comfort zone when...
well, when you feel uncomfortable.

Same Side

Respecting each other even when you are exhausted, always remaining on the same side of any problem – that's what love is.

Being on the same side means that you both want a healthy, happy relationship.

Remaining Open

Conflict is not always to be avoided. When you are honest with one another, at times, there will be conflict. You will argue.

Conflict awakens defensiveness. Be very careful: being defensive shuts down curiosity. And there is no effective communication without curiosity.

Don't Run - Practice

In conflict, ask questions – genuine questions, not rhetorical. Slow down to listen to each other. Having an argument faster will not improve the outcome, nor will it end sooner.

If you don't like to argue, then learn to do it well. Learn to work together to solve problems. If you don't like to argue, avoiding conflict is the worst idea.

Not running from conflict, even when we hate conflict - that's what love is.

Same Side

Battles can be won but problems cannot be solved from adversarial positions. You can still disagree and be on the same side as long as you remember that you are both there to care for your relationship.

In good times, in bad and all times in between, what you must always have in common is that you both are caring for your relationship. (This is difficult. When the time comes, you may need to get some help with this one.)

When to Be Quiet

When you can see and feel only adversarial relationship with your partner, shhhhhhhh, be very quiet. Reach out, get support. This is very important.

Knowing when to shut up, knowing when to stop, knowing when to get help – that's what love is.

How We Learn

Do you remember learning to drive a standard shift car or to play a musical instrument – or ride a bicycle? Anything that at first seems impossible but, with practice, becomes second nature. Mastering effective communication skills is like that.

Understanding the concept of where your fingers go on the keyboard is one thing; getting those fingers to cooperate with your brain is quite another.

Practice, Repeat, Practice

How long will it take to learn this or learn that? When something is difficult, there really is no way to say exactly how long it will take. But we absolutely know exactly how we will learn: practice, repetitious practice.

Lessons from the very best teachers do not create mastery. Only practice can do that.

Foundation of Flaws

The foundation for healthy communication is understanding that we are all flawed, that we all have more to learn and that we must be willing to admit when we are wrong. In a word: humility.

Humility is that place where we recognize we are not better than others – and we are not worse. The second part of that is harder for many.

Humility is the common meeting ground where we understand that we all have much more in common than we are different.

Changing for the Relationship

Mastering relationship skills is not for the faint of heart. Effective communication, especially in times of conflict, calls for a focused dedication and repetitious practice. It calls for honest self-evaluation, humility, a sense of fair play and a willingness to change according to the needs of the relationship.

Unlearning

To learn to communicate effectively, you may have some unlearning to do. Most of us have some pretty dysfunctional relationship habits that will need to change. Unlearning is hard, maybe the hardest part.

Letting go of our old default settings is absolutely necessary if we are to learn to communicate effectively.

Patience

One promise we need to make to each other is to be patient when working on improving communication. In fact, patience is an invaluable communication tool.

In healthy communication, we take turns. Simple but very easy to forget. And when it is not your turn to talk, it is your turn to listen.

Catch

A good conversation is like a game of catch in which the ball is tossed back and forth, back and forth, each person catching and tossing.

Don't be a ball hog. Avoid using your turn to lecture. Keep your eyes on your partner so you are less likely to forget that there are two of you in the conversation.

Don't Sell ~ Converse

And don't be a salesman, using your turn to make a case for your partner being wrong and you being right. Say what you are thinking, say what you are feeling. Be honest, be clear, and whenever possible, be brief.

Conversation is dialogue,
not alternating monologues.
Back and forth, back and forth.

A Coupe of Don'ts

Ask questions with curiosity. Rhetorical questions are dangerous.

Beware of sarcasm. It can be fun when we are playing, when we are being silly but in serious conversations, sarcasm is dangerous.

Sarcasm is often the conversation-ending bayonet of the desperate communicator. Much better to put down that weapon down.

Future Orient

When you describe a problem that you are having, don't stop at the problem definition. Say something about what you want, about how you hope your relationship can change. Think of this a future-orienting. Much better to look forward than to become stuck in looking back.

Implementation

We learn from the past, practice what we have learned so that we can create our best future. Being committed to learning and to implementing what we learn to improve communication, that's what love is.

How much of what you say you have learned have you put to good use? Keep challenging yourself with this question.

Intimacy

Love is not love until love is vulnerable.
-Theodore Roethke

In-To-Me-See

Strategy is the opposite of intimacy. Strategy involves second-guessing, anticipating responses, plans A, B & C and even manipulating each other.

Intimacy is direct and honest. Intimacy takes guts.

Authentic love is not strategic.
It is intimate.

Being Safe

We want our closest relationship to be the safest relationship in the whole world. We want our closest relationship to be our emotional home, the place where we can leave our protective armor on the front porch and enter as our true selves.

Intimacy makes this possible. Being respectfully honest with each other, while it is very hard work, is what will keep our relationships clean - clear of debris from a past ignored.

Extra Armor

When we are not careful, the opposite can come to be. We can feel the need to don additional armor as we go through the front door. Not good but it can happen. Neither panic nor ignore. Find help.

Reaching out for help demonstrates strength, not weakness.

One Important Rule

Here is the best policy about getting help: if either of you believe it is a good idea, then do it. More than likely one partner will be more reluctant than the other when this happens. Better to have the policy in place. Either one of you can initiate getting help for your relationship. The other agrees to come along, like it or not.

Don't make getting help a last resort.
Early detection makes
for excellent prognosis.

Important Rules

You do not need too many rules in a healthy relationship, no complicated policy manual required. But the rules that need to be there are extremely important.

Beware of unspoken rules from your parent's relationship creeping into yours. Unspoken rules are dangerous.

Rules for Us All

Of course, you may have rules unique to your relationship but here are rules you will be wise to include.

No yelling, no screaming, no violent verbal energy. And the sounds of our voices can be violent. Take care in not just what you say but also how you say it.

No name calling. None. Don't do it.

If what I call being emphatic is perceived by my partner as yelling, then I need to stop "yelling."

Play Fair

No threatening to leave the relationship during an intense discussion or fight. Threatening to leave in times like this is always counter-productive. If you need to talk about separating, do that in a separate conversation.

Threatening to leave in the middle of an argument is not fair; It's cheating. It is like holding your relationship hostage.

It can be a good idea to write a list of your worst communication flaws & share them with each other.

Boat Rocking

An honest, intimate relationship cannot be ruled by the principle of "don't rock the boat." The boat will need to be rocked now and then if we don't want it to capsize later.

Being respectfully honest, keeping our emotional home clean is extremely important.

Understanding that rocking a boat is much better than sinking it. Sometimes courageous boat rocking is what love is.

Lessons in Giving & Receiving

Love teaches us how to give but it also teaches us how to receive. Sometimes that is the harder lesson to learn. Sometimes we are much much better at giving love than we are at receiving love.

For some people, giving love feels great but receiving love is difficult, sometimes even painful.

Learn to Receive

You may want to retreat, thinking that giving is enough, that receiving is not all that important. Sometimes we are even taught that receiving is bad, that it makes us selfish or that we are undeserving. This is not true.

Beware of negative arrogance –
the belief that you are uniquely less
deserving than others.

Let Yourself Be Loved

Consider what you feel when someone you love will not let your love in – when they refuse to believe that you care as much as you do, when they cannot see the beauty in themselves that you see so clearly.

Then consider how you feel when you love someone and they know it, when you love someone and they really feel it, when they accept your love.

Receiving love that is genuinely offered is the gift you give the giver.

Your Responsibility

One more time for good measure: When your partner loves you and you can fully accept that love, even if it is difficult, you are both receiving and giving a gift.

If letting yourself be loved is difficult, it is your responsibility to practice until it is not. One partner feeling less deserving than another is no small matter. It will create problems.

Giving love but not receiving love is not a higher road. Sometimes letting love in takes guts.

No Fair to Run

Letting the love in may feel risky. You may feel vulnerable and you may want to run as fast as you can to the familiar landscape of giving-but-not-receiving. But, in love, that simply is not fair.

Both giving and receiving
– that's what love is.

Caring for Love

The way to love anything is to realize that it may be lost.
-Gilbert Chesterton

Becoming

Love is about becoming the person you want to be. Contrary to some opinions, it is not about giving up any part of yourself. Love is full of opportunities to be better people, to be the best version of ourselves.

In love we become more, not less.

Compromise & Sacrifice

Love includes a willingness to compromise and even to sacrifice but it is important not to mistake this truth for an EQUATION that too many of us are taught in one form or another. That equation is *love = sacrifice*. This equation teaches us that no act of love is genuine unless there is sacrifice. This is not true.

Sacrificing and compromising are not the only ways to love.

Don't Let Go of You

Remember: receiving is an essential part of being in a loving relationship. It is not necessary that you give up what is important to you as an individual, in order to be in a happy, successful relationship.

Think "win – win"
And follow your dreams.

Balance Over Time

The balance of who is compromising and sacrificing at any given time may not feel right to us. It may not always feel fair. The challenge is to manage this balance over time. If we expect everything to be 50/50 at all times, we will be very disappointed.

Be the best part of yourself on both yours and your partner's behalf.

Protect from Resentment

To allow an important dream to atrophy or even to die is not good for a relationship. There is a danger of resentment. But even if not resentment, you will have unnecessarily given away an important part of yourself.

If your partner has difficulty supporting your dream, be patient, but don't give up on yourself. Don't give up on your partner either.

Take Care

The best kind of person to be in a relationship with is someone who takes excellent care of themselves. Think of it as someone who picks up their own emotional socks, who does their own emotional dishes, so that someone else does not have to do it for them.

Trusting your partner to take good care can be a great relief, a real energy saver.

Positive Selfishness

Contrary to what many of us have been taught, there is such a thing as positive selfishness. Positive selfishness is a compassionate focus on yourself that not only will not harm others, it will actually benefit others.

Sometimes to take care of yourself you will need to disappoint others.

Be Careful, Be Honest

This is a bit tricky: To hurt someone's feelings is not necessarily the same as causing harm. We all need tolerance for not getting our way.

Be very honest with yourself and with your partner about whether or not you have sustained injury from disappointment.

This distinction must never be used against one another. You do not get to tell your partner how they feel nor do they get to tell you how you feel.

Only Mutual Respect

Be careful to not think of respect in terms of either/or. Respect in a relationship must be mutual. It will not work any other way.

Genuine respect for your partner begins with self-respect. Do not forget this.

Being someone who respects your partner, being a self-caring, self-respecting person – that's what love is.

No Mystery

Love is proactive, not passive. It does not just happen. It does not simply come and go according to its own mysterious plan. Love is about both how we feel and what we do. BOTH.

With great love, comes great responsibility

Regular Maintenance

Love may come intact, beautiful and shiny, like a brand-new car, but it will not maintain itself any more than your new car will.

Happily-ever-after is something you create together, something you make and maintain, not something that just happens. We call all say those words. Putting those words into action, that's what love is.

Nothing for Granted

If love just happened, if love was self-sustaining, it would not be special. And we would, of course, take it for granted.

The practice of gratitude is very possibly the most important thing to know. Without gratitude, love will deteriorate.

Essential Kindness

Kindness is gratitude's companion. Don't wait for kindness to show up when you are having a good day. Make kindness a part of your worst days. Not just with each other. The practice of conscious kindness makes us better people. Being a better person makes your relationship stronger.

Living from gratitude and kindness, that's what love is.

Commitment

Love involves commitment, not just for the purposes of great sounding wedding vows. The commitment love calls for is strong, energetic and resilient. True commitment is a daily practice.

Commitment is the real source of happily-ever-after.

More & Less

Love as a feeling for one another may come and go. Some days are better than others. Yes, that's right, from the emotional perspective, you may love your partner less today than you will this time next week, or vice versa. Nothing to be scared about; this is perfectly normal.

Pay Attention

It is not realistic to expect that you will feel exactly the same about each other every single day of your life.

This does not mean that you don't need to pay attention. Never take any of this for granted.

How about this for a daily practice: paying attention.

An Important Distinction

Sometimes feeling less love is a part of the ebb and flow or your feelings in the relationship. Sometimes feeling less love can endanger commitment and that is a problem. If that is happening, do not delay in asking for help.

Treat your love as the precious gift it is. If you feel it fade, ask yourself, "What have I forgotten?" or "What am I forgetting?"

Appropriate Caution

Love as a commitment is steadfast and unchanging. Commitment is the solid steel and concrete foundation of your healthy relationship.

Again, never take the maintenance of this foundation for granted. You do not need to obsessively guard the foundation of commitment but neither should you ever be without appropriate caution.

Feelings will vary but commitment must be constant.

One Day at a Time

The alcoholic in recovery remains committed to not taking a drink even on days when drinking sounds like a pretty good idea. Such is the commitment of relationship.

On some days you may not feel particularly loving, or even like staying in the relationship. Commitment reminds you to stay, to do whatever you need to do to take good care of yourself, but not to violate the foundation of your relationship.

Commitment is what love is.
Caring for commitment is what love is.

There Are No Breaks

Love is about shared responsibility, understanding that our relationships require both partners' attention. It will not work to come and go from your responsibility. We don't take breaks from love.

When there are problems to solve, remember that you are on the same side, problem solvers with a common goal.

Sharing

It is also very important to remember that we cannot solve multiple problems simultaneously. When there is more than one problem to solve, take turns.

Sharing responsibility is like sharing anything else. It requires patience, respect, flexibility and kindness. And more patience.

*Never underestimate
the importance of being fair.*

Lab Partners

Think of yourselves as lab partners in this big chemistry experiment called life.

Lab partners work together to solve problems; they don't work against one another.

Being lab partners, solving problems together with respect and kindness. And have I mentioned patience? That's what love is.

Blame Is A Mistake

Smart problem solvers are vitally interested in responsibility but have little interest in one particular concept that has tremendous potential to seriously trip us up. That concept is blame.

Assigning blame and taking responsibility are not the same. Not at all.

Invest Wisely

Responsibility and blame are not the same. When we are investing energy making a case for blame, we are usually working overtime to relieve ourselves of that same blame.

We might think the best way to avoid blame is to blame someone or something else. In loving relationships, that is not the best way to do anything.

Forward Ho!

Blame only anchors us to the past. Responsibility propels us forward. Blame is a distraction. Responsibility is a way to focus.

Learn from the past,
then get the hell out of there.

Live in the present
and look to the future.

Remind Each Other

Lab partners who love each other need to remind themselves frequently of the difference between blame and responsibility. It is easy to forget. It is dangerous to forget.

Knowing the difference between blame and responsibility – that's what love is.

Humility

The art of being wise is the art of knowing what to overlook.
-William James

Blah Blah

Blah blah blah. Blah blah blah. And blah. Yada yada ya ya blah blah ya. It is important for us to recognize when talking is counterproductive. And sometimes we prefer quiet.

When Quiet Is Wisdom

Sometimes you will not know what to say. Sometimes there will be no way to say what you need to say.

Sometimes you will just need time to consider, to think, to feel but not speak.

Sometimes when you are speaking, you will become aware that you should not be. Here is what to do on those occasions: stop speaking.

Having the courage to sit in silence when you have no idea what to say – that's what love is.

Exactly Wrong

Sometimes you will fill the silence with the exact wrong words. Sometimes we all say things we should not.

We learn to know when to stop, when to decide to do no more damage. There will be times when we must know when to shut up.

Having the wisdom to sit in silence when you want to say the wrong thing – that's what love is.

*Sometimes silence is
the best way to love.*

Takes Time

Learning when it is best to risk saying something that might be treacherous and when to err toward caution is something that might take a couple of decades. Always in school, never graduating - that's what love is.

It is wise to know when and how to quit while you are behind.

Apology

Genuine apologies are essential; apologies to sweep differences under the carpet are dangerous.

When you apologize, know what you are apologizing for.

Genuine Apology

Understand that an apology does not mean your partner will no longer be hurt or angry. A genuine apology means that you understand why they are hurt or angry.

Your apology must come with a willingness to not be forgiven immediately. Read that sentence again.

Problematic Apology

Apologies without amends are not apologies. An apology too often repeated stops being an apology and becomes a part of the problem.

Understanding that apologies are sacred – that's what love is.

Forgiveness

Genuine forgiveness is essential; forgiveness to sweep differences under the carpet is dangerous.

When you forgive, know what you are forgiving. Be able and willing to say what you are forgiving.

False Forgiveness

Being forgiving is a wonderful thing. Forgiving insincerely is not forgiveness.

Forgiving because you automatically assume things are always your fault is a problem that you had better not ignore.

Genuine Forgiveness

Ultimately forgiveness is not so much something we do as it is our natural state when we are honest and do not hold on to old pain.

Forgiveness is the willingness to let go of what needs to be let go. Letting go when that is the right thing to do – that's what love is.

Forgiveness is sacred.

Strange Dream

Describing love is like trying to tell someone about a strange dream: "You were there in the dream," we might say, "but you weren't really you. And we were in San Francisco, but somehow near Times Square."

Love Has Range

Sometimes love is deeply serious, sometimes it is fun, sometimes it is difficult, sometimes it is hilarious. Enjoy how many different words can describe your love.

Sometimes love is just about being with each other, with or without words. Sometimes we receive the gift of a glimpse of pure unconditional love.

Sometimes love just is.

Intangible

Sometimes love is indescribable. Sometimes the perfect words are there. Sometimes you get to say just the right thing.

Often love is confusing, frustrating and even discouraging. Sometimes love hides from us. But it is always here, somewhere.

Not knowing where love is – that is very scary. Try not to panic.

Courage

You do not have to feel brave to be brave. And being brave does not mean you do not need support.

Reaching out for support certainly takes more guts than isolating with your fears.

Courage doesn't just happen.
We can choose to be courageous.

Remembering

Love can be lost but never destroyed. When love goes missing, never stop looking. Try looking where you first discovered it. That is, remember when you first met, remember when you fell in love.

When you have misplaced love, remember times when it was fully present. Remember with your mind and your heart and your whole being.

Never giving up.
Always remembering -
that's what love is.

Renewal

Love needs to be renewed. Love needs fresh air. And fresh ideas. Love is creative. Love is interesting because it is about being interested in each other.

You might lose interest because you think you know everything there is to know about your partner – but you don't.

Sometimes We Do Know

When you begin to think that you know your partner better than they know themselves, it is important that you remember that you do not.

There will be times when you will believe that you know what your partner is thinking better than they do. Sometimes you might be right.

That makes things confusing. Do not make the mistake of thinking you will always be right.

Being Honest

When your partner does not trust what you say and is actually correct in saying what you really mean, then you are not being honest. Change that. Do not let pride get in your way.

It really is okay to say, "I think you are right. That was what I was thinking."

No surprise here:
being honest – that's what love is.

Time

There is one essential ingredient in love that, if we are not careful, we will misplace. That ingredient is time.

We say there is not enough time. And later we may regret not having taken the time. But there is enough time. If there is not, go make some more.

Time moves only in one direction.
And it speeds up as we get older.
Remember your daily practice of
paying attention.

Time Is a Gift

When someone says that there is not enough time, do not believe it. Time is limited but there is enough if we use it consciously – wisely.

Time's limitation is what makes it a priority. Time's limitation is what makes it such a special gift.

Giving the gift of time,
honoring the value of time,
making time for each other -
that's what love is.

Our Nature

Such is our nature: I wonder, I search, I discover, I learn, I know, I forget, I wonder, I search, I discover, I learn, I know, I forget, I wonder…

We are human beings.
We are forgetting machines.

Post-It Notes

Do not waste time and energy expecting a better memory. Create a life full of reminders. We need post-it notes to jog our memories, to remind us to make the most of our time.

We can all be each other's post-it's. We can remind each other to stay awake, to not take each other for granted.

Maybe instead of saying hello when we walk to the street we could greet each other with "Wake Up!"

Regret-Reduction

It is important that we remember that we might not know when the last time will be.

Live life, love each other according to the regret-reduction program – living each day in a way you are least likely to regret.

Reminders

Fill your life with reminders that love is a daily practice, reminders that mistakes are opportunities to improve how we love, reminders about how to love.

Creating reminders, remembering
what is most important –
that's what love is.

Using This Book

*I cannot promise to fix all your problems but I can promise
you won't face them alone.*

-Stephen King

Read It Again

If you like what you have read, if you have learned something or been reminded of something you had forgotten, read this book again.

Read it again. After all, repetition is the key to mastery. Repetition is the key to mastery.

Repetition is the key to mastery.
Repetition is the key to mastery.
Repetition is the key to mastery.

Just Open the Book

If you like what you have read, keep this book handy.

Open to any page and you will find a reminder, a Post-It Note. Maybe you will find exactly what you need to remember at that particular time on that particular day.

Where We Started

Now that you have read this little book... use it. Remember where we started: love is more about action than feeling.

If love is not demonstrated, then it is not love. Put what you are learning here and what you are remembering here into practice.

Practice won't make perfect.
There is no perfect.
Practice means daily practice.

A Twist

This looks like a gift book but that is not what it really is. It is a workbook.

All the blank space is for you, for your notes and scribbles about what you know about what love is, about what you want your love to be.

Choosing how you will love
— that's what love is.

Choices we make every
day of our lives
— that's what love is.

What Love Is

Love is a choice. Love is an opportunity. Love is a responsibility. Love is a gift. Love is a challenge. Love is beautiful and painful and confusing and redeeming and hilarious and excruciating and mysterious and boring and exciting and did I mention confusing?

It Is What You Decide

Really it is just this: love is what you decide, love is what you make it to be. Love does not just happen.

We make love happen.

ABOUT THE AUTHOR

Thom Rutledge is a psychotherapist and has been working with individuals, groups and couples for 35 years. He has been featured on NBC's Today Show, Anderson Cooper 360, The Fox Network, Australia's Channel 10  and has consulted with The Dr. Phil Show.

Thom has been married to Dede Beasley (the well-known Experiential Equine Counselor) for 32 years and they live on a small farm just outside of Nashville, Tennessee.

BOOKS BY THOM RUTLEDGE

Embracing Fear
The Greater Possibilities
The Self-Forgiveness Handbook
Earning Your Own Respect
Simple Truth
If I Were They
Nutshell Essays, Volume 1
Nutshell Essays, Volume 2
The Recovery Decision
Life Without Ed (w/ Jenni Schaefer)

BOOKS   WORKSHOPS
PROFESSIONAL TRAINING
KEYNOTE SPEAKING
TREATMENT PROGRAM CONSULTATION
IN-OFFICE PSYCHOTHERAPY
TELEPHONE & SKYPE CONSULTATIONS
SELF-HELP JOURNALING
WWW.FACEBOOK.COM/THOM.RUTLEDGE.9
TWITTER: @THOMRUTLEDGE

WWW.THOMRUTLEDGE.COM
THOMRUTLEDGEAUTHOR@GMAIL.COM

<u>WHAT DO YOU SAY LOVE IS?</u>

If you would like to be considered as a possible contributor to a sequel to this book, send us your own concise description of What Love Is. Contributions need to be brief, clear and to the point. And please send no more than 3 submissions. Please understand that we are not certain there will be a follow up book and that if there is, your submissions will be considered but not necessarily used. We will contact you when/if we begin work on this project. Thank you. And thank you for purchasing *What Love Is*. Your support is never taken for granted.

Email submissions to
thomrutledgeauthor@gmail.com
with "Submission" in the subject line.

One More Thing

Wait. Before you go, one more thing. Extremely important. In fact, tear this page out and carry it with you.

Laughter. Humor. Just because something is serious, even sacred, that does not mean it is not also, at times, hilarious.

Serious and funny are not opposites. Very often they need each other. And you will need them both.

Laughing together
– that's what love is.

See other side for wisdom

(Did you think I was kidding? Seriously, tear this page out and keep it with you.)

Benediction

What lies behind you and what lies in front of you
pales in comparison to what lies inside you.

-Ralph Waldo Emerson

May we remember and respect our
human imperfection. May we remember
and respect our divine perfection.

And may we never confuse the two.

Thank you to Dede for being – and for loving me.

Thank you to all my clients who have trusted me with their relationships.

Thank you to Leigh Robbins and Ken Barken for the original assignment.

Thank you to Mark Smith for snapping the photo of what love is.

Thank you to Jules for being a loving friend and for reading this first – many times.

Thank you to Natalie Soriano for last minute assist.

Special thanks to Sylvan. Always.

Thom Rutledge
331 22nd Ave North, Suite One
Nashville, TN 37203

www.thomrutledge.com
thomrutledgeauthor@gmail.com

If you have enjoyed & benefited from <u>What Love Is</u>, you will also like <u>The Greater Possibilities</u>.

The power of true success is revealed when we can see past our daily distractions, setting illusion aside in favor of the real magic that emerges from deep within us. Only then will we discover the greater possibilities.

-from The Introduction

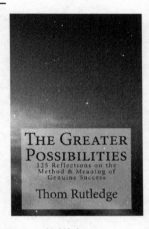

<u>DISCOUNTS & SIGNED COPIES</u>
If you are interested in a discount when ordering 30 or more copies of either *The Greater Possibilities* or *What Love Is*, to give as gifts, email **thomrutledgeauthor@gmail.com** for more information. Also, let us know if you would like books signed by author.

51811623R00097

Made in the USA
Middletown, DE
14 November 2017